Sally's Story

the dodo

Sally's Story

How the Tiniest Puppy
Learned to Breathe on Her Own

BY BONNIE BADER

SCHOLASTIC INC.

Photo credits: Cover: all images © Kathryn Mongrain; photo insert pages 1–3: © Kathryn Mongrain; photo insert page 4 (top): © Kathryn Mongrain; photo insert page 4 (bottom): © Bonnie Acosta-Schmeisser; photo insert pages 5–8: © Bonnie Acosta-Schmeisser; photo insert background: © Shutterstock.com; page design elements: © Shutterstock.com

ISBN 978-1-5461-1463-5

10 9 8 7 6 5 4 3 2 1   24 25 26 27 28

Printed in the U.S.A.   40
First printing 2024
Book design by Jennifer Rinaldi

CONTENTS

CHAPTER 1
A CALL FOR HELP

DING! DING!

Kathryn Mongrain's alarm rang. She opened one eye to look at her phone. It was 3 p.m. on January 2, 2022.

Kat was about to get out of bed when she realized today was her day off. She worked as a licensed veterinary technician at an emergency animal hospital near Houston, Texas. Her usual shift was 5 p.m. to 5 a.m. But today, she could sleep in.

"Kat!" her husband, Devin, called from the other room. "Are you awake? It's your turn to take Hammy!"

Kat shot up in bed. *Of course!* Even though she wasn't working her regular job today, she still had her other job to do—and that was taking care of animals right there in her home!

She quickly brushed her teeth, dressed, and rushed into the dining room. That was where Kat and Devin had set up a nursery for special needs puppies and kittens. The room was also the headquarters of their nonprofit organization, The Bottle Brigade—named for the many tiny babies they rescued who needed to be fed by bottle at first.

Kat scanned the room, which was filled with the equipment she used to help the animals she brought in. She had four incubators, pens with heating pads, bottles, medicine, and more. Kat smiled when she saw the photos hanging on the walls of many animals they had helped save. Most of the animals Kat took in were clinging to life. Some had pneumonia, a sickness that affects the lungs and makes it hard to breathe. Others came in with a cleft palate, which is a hole in the roof of their mouth that makes it difficult for them to eat. Kat thought about all the animals she had cared for who now had loving homes.

Eek, eek! A high-pitched squealing noise interrupted Kat's thought. It was Hammy, a little puppy she had recently taken in.

"My, you sure are noisy today," Kat teased.

She walked over to the incubator where Hammy was curled up and staying nice and warm.

Kat smiled at Hammy. When she first rescued him, he was barely breathing and not making any noise at all. Now he was yelping with joy all the time!

"Have you fed Hammy yet?" Kat asked Devin.

Devin shook his head sleepily. He had been up every two hours overnight and then all day while Kat slept.

"I was just about to, but now that you're up, I'll leave the feeding to you," he said with a yawn.

Kat took the feeding tube from her husband and reached into the incubator to pick up Hammy.

"You get some sleep," she told Devin.

Devin kissed Kat on the top of her head and shuffled off to bed.

"How are you feeling, baby?" Kat asked as she nuzzled Hammy.

Hammy stared at Kat with his brown eyes and then settled into sucking Kat's finger as she fed him.

The rest of the afternoon went as it usually did: Kat checked on and fed the two other animals she and Devin were caring for. Then she took out her phone to film the animals. Kat liked to post videos on social media. The Bottle Brigade had a big following! Plus, once the animals were adopted, Kat gave the forever families videos and photos of their pet's earliest days.

Just as Kat was putting her feet up for a

moment, her phone rang. It was a call from her friend, Hilarie Rogers, another animal rescuer.

Kat listened carefully to Hilarie, concern clouding her blue eyes.

While Kat was on the phone, Devin returned to the nursery after his nap. He saw the look on Kat's face.

"Everything okay?" Devin asked after Kat ended her call. The couple was used to receiving emergency calls at all times of day. And they were also used to getting little to no sleep!

"Hilarie just got a call from a breeder who has a very sick puppy," Kat began. "She's having trouble breathing. The breeder wasn't willing to take on a puppy with her condition. But luckily, they knew Hilarie and gave her a call."

"And Hilarie called you," Devin finished. In their local rescue community, others knew that The Bottle Brigade had incubators and other equipment to help animals who were ill. Not all rescue organizations had that kind of special equipment.

Kat nodded, twirling a strand of long brown hair around her finger.

"Something tells me you're more concerned than usual," Devin said.

Kat was used to taking in rescues and helping them. But there was something different about this puppy.

"This puppy can't breathe," Kat told Devin. "Hilarie doesn't know if she'll make it. She called me as the last resort."

They both knew that it was a thirty-minute drive from Spring, Texas, where the breeder was located, to their home, which was just outside Houston. Kat and Devin desperately hoped the puppy would survive the trip.

The light brown puppy with little floppy ears shivered in the car, even though she was wrapped in blankets.

I c-can't b-breathe, the tiny puppy thought. *Where is my mama? Where are my brothers and sisters? And where is this lady taking me? I need some air. Help me, please!*

After Kat had received the call, she began to pace nervously around her home, waiting for the puppy to arrive. The minutes crept by so slowly.

"Why don't you sit down for a bit?" Devin suggested. "You're going to be plenty busy when the puppy gets here."

Kat nodded. "And why don't you try to catch some more sleep? I'll wake you if I need your help."

Devin agreed and returned to bed.

Kat looked at her phone and realized it was time to bottle-feed another one of her puppies. She gently lifted the dog out of the incubator and sank into her couch, a warm bottle of milk in her hand. She closed her eyes and took a deep breath to ease her nerves as the tiny puppy in her arms suckled on the bottle. Kat had helped save so many animals over the past few years. Hopefully, she would have the chance to save this new puppy, too.

Just then, one of Kat's dogs, Etta, walked over to where Kat was sitting and put her head in Kat's lap. Each time Kat looked at Etta, she was filled with hope. She remembered Etta as a sickly little Great Dane puppy whose back feet didn't work. Now she was a *huge* dog who loved to romp around. Kat knew that Etta wanted to play, so she picked up a ball and threw it to the other side of the room. Etta scampered after it, bringing the ball back to Kat. Again and again, Kat tossed the ball, but the entire time, her mind was on the little puppy who was struggling to breathe.

CHAPTER 2

BLUE BABY

AT LAST, KAT HEARD A CAR PULL into her driveway. She rushed outside and saw the breeder lifting a tiny bundle out of her car.

"Oh my gosh!" Kat exclaimed, looking at the puppy. "She's blue!" The puppy's gums and tongue should have been a warm pink color, but both were blue. Kat knew that the blue color was a sign that there wasn't enough oxygen getting to the puppy's lungs.

The breeder nodded. "But she's still alive," she said.

Kat rushed inside with the puppy and carefully unwrapped the blankets. This puppy was so teeny she fit into the palm of Kat's hand.

Kat quickly lowered the puppy into an oxygen bubble. The bubble was box shaped, with blue walls and a soft plastic window in the front. The plastic window had a zipper around it so Kat could easily get the puppy in and out. Inside the bubble, Kat had put a ton of comfy blankets and a soft stuffed teddy bear. There was also a small tube that pumped oxygen. Hopefully, the oxygen would help the puppy breathe. Breathing in oxygen was the only way the puppy would survive.

"I'm so glad you got her here in time," Kat said.

"And I'm so glad you could take her in," the breeder said.

The two women watched in silence as the puppy took in the oxygen with short little gasps.

"Do you know what's wrong with her?" Kat asked, breaking the silence.

"It's likely pneumonia," the breeder said. "The vet thought she probably aspirated on her mother's milk."

Aspiration happens when liquid or food is inhaled instead of swallowed. The liquid gets into the lungs and an infection—in this case pneumonia—can occur.

Kat looked over at Hammy, who had also come to her with pneumonia. Thankfully, he was now breathing on his own. Kat hoped for the same outcome with this new little puppy.

Once the breeder had left, Kat gave Hilarie a call. "Thanks for calling me," she told her friend. "I'm going to do what I do with all my babies: try to save her."

"Thanks again for taking this one in, Kat," Hilarie replied. "I know you'll do your best with her."

Now all Kat could do was wait to see if the oxygen would help.

Where am I now? the puppy thought, gazing at Kat from inside the bubble. *And what are these little puffs of air coming out of this tube? Gasp! Gasp! I need to suck up the little puffs. In and out. In and out. These little puffs are helping. I*

can breathe a bit better now. But it's still so hard.
I have to concentrate a lot: in and out, in and out.

Kat watched as the little blue puppy struggled to take in the oxygen. Kat hoped being inside the bubble would help.

The puppy was a teeny-tiny dachshund (say: DOCKS-hund.) Some people call a dachshund a "wiener dog" because their body is so long—just like a wiener, or a hot dog! Originally, dachshunds were bred as hunting dogs, but today they are popular pets. There are three types of dachshunds: smooth-haired, wire-haired, or long-haired. This one was long-haired.

Just then, Devin walked into the nursery. "I see our new patient has arrived," he said with a yawn.

"She has," Kat said. "I'm hoping the oxygen will help revive her."

"Pneumonia?" Devin asked.

Kat nodded.

"Can you see anything else wrong with her?" Devin wondered aloud.

Kat shook her head. "Not right now. Hilarie said the breeder was pretty sure the puppy wasn't born with a birth defect. She was nursing well for the first two weeks of her life. But I won't be one hundred percent sure until I do a full examination. All I want her to do right now is breathe comfortably."

Kat and Devin had taken in lots of animals with pneumonia. But none had been this blue on arrival. Kat knew that inside the puppy's body, her red blood cells should be carrying oxygen to different parts of her body. But her blood had lost much of its oxygen, which is why her tongue and gums had turned a bluish color.

As Kat and Devin took care of the three other animals in their nursery, they kept a close eye on the puppy in the bubble.

Breathe in. Breathe out. The puppy worked hard to fill her lungs with air. *Breathe in. Breathe . . . hey, this is getting easier and easier! And I'm starting to feel a bit better, too. But I'm still scared. Where is my mama?*

About thirty minutes later, Kat walked over to the bubble, where she got a big surprise. The puppy's little tongue was pink.

"It's helping!" she shouted. "The oxygen is working!"

Devin ran over to the bubble and hugged Kat tightly.

"I think we have a little fighter here," he told her.

"I hope so," Kat said, her eyes tearing up. "I really hope so."

CHAPTER 3
FEEDING AND BREATHING

NOW THAT THE PUPPY WAS breathing easier, Kat had to figure out how to feed her. Hopefully, the puppy would take a bottle.

Kat knew that since this tiny puppy didn't have access to her mother's milk, she would have to make a bottle of puppy formula. The formula had all the nutrients and vitamins the puppy needed to grow. But the puppy also needed medicine to fight the pneumonia. As a licensed vet tech, Kat had exactly what the puppy needed right there in her home nursery. Kat would mix some medicine in with the formula. This would help fight off the infection in her lungs and help open her airways to better take in oxygen.

Kat mixed up a bottle of formula with warm water and then dropped a bit on her wrist to make sure it wasn't too hot. She also checked that the bottle's nipple had a small hole, just large enough for the milk to slowly drip out. If the milk came out too quickly, the puppy could choke.

Kat's plan was to take the puppy out of the bubble and hold her so the puppy's stomach was resting on Kat's hands. It was also important that her head was upright so the milk could go down easily.

Slowly, Kat opened one side of the bubble and stuck in her hand. She made sure the puppy was on her stomach, with her head upright.

"Hello, little one," Kat said softly. "How are you feeling today?"

But as soon as Kat took the puppy out of the plastic cube, she began to gasp for air!

"Oh no!" Kat exclaimed. She quickly returned the puppy to the safety of the oxygen-filled bubble.

"Talking to the animals again?" Devin asked with a smile.

Kat gave him a serious look.

"We have a big problem here," she said. "As

soon as I took her out, she couldn't breathe. I need to figure out how to help her breathe and eat at the same time."

Devin looked puzzled. "Hmmm, usually once an animal has been taking in the oxygen for a while, they can come out of the bubble for a bit. But I guess this one's lungs are weaker than we initially thought."

Kat nodded sadly. "I'll try again. Maybe if I open the bubble just enough to fit the bottle in, most of the oxygen will stay in the bubble."

But as soon as Kat opened the bubble and stuck the bottle inside, the puppy began to gasp for air.

"This isn't working, either," Kat said, hanging her head.

As Kat sat there trying to figure out what

to do, Etta came up to her and put her big head in Kat's lap.

"Etta," Kat said, "it's time to come up with a different plan."

I am so hungry! the puppy thought. *Where is my mama? Who is going to give me milk? I see another dog around here—maybe she'll feed me!*

"I think our only choice is to put in a feeding tube," Kat told Devin.

"But that means you'll have to take her to the hospital," Devin noted.

Kat nodded. She knew that to put in the feeding tube correctly, she needed an X-ray to make sure the tube was properly in place. And since she didn't have an X-ray machine at her home, she had to take the puppy to the hospital.

"Right," Kat told her husband. "And the sooner the better."

Kat grabbed her car keys, picked up the bubble with the puppy inside, and rushed out the door.

"Don't worry, little one," Kat told the puppy as she pulled up to the hospital. "Just one little procedure and you'll feel better. I promise."

Kat parked her car, took the bubble out of the car, and hurried into the hospital.

"Another baby?" one of the technicians asked Kat.

Kat nodded. "Yes. And this one needs a feeding tube—fast. I haven't been able to bottle-feed her because she can't be out of the bubble, even for a minute!" Kat explained.

"Let me give you a hand," the tech offered

as Kat walked into a room that had an X-ray machine.

Although Kat had a lot of experience putting in feeding tubes, she knew that in this case, she would have to work very quickly. She didn't want the puppy to be without oxygen for long, so an extra pair of hands would be helpful.

Kat lifted the puppy out of the bubble and gave her a quick kiss on her nose. "This won't take long, and it won't hurt. Although it might be the teensiest bit uncomfortable."

Once the tube was inserted, Kat put the puppy back in the bubble so she could breathe comfortably for a few minutes.

Then Kat walked over to the X-ray machine. She needed to take a quick image of the puppy's tummy to make sure the end of the feeding tube was in the correct position.

The tube needed to carry food directly into the puppy's stomach.

Gently taking the puppy from the bubble once again, Kat hurried over to the X-ray machine. "One, two, three!" The machine buzzed and recorded the image.

"Here, let me take her back to the bubble," the tech offered, noticing that the puppy was starting to gasp for air.

"Just a sec," Kat said. She quickly taped the other end of the tube to the top of the puppy's head so she wouldn't be able to play with it and pull it out.

Once the puppy had settled back into her bubble, Kat connected the puppy's feeding tube to another flexible tube that was inside the bubble. A small section of the plastic piping peeked outside the bubble, allowing Kat to drip food and medication into one end. The food Kat put in traveled down the tube directly into the puppy's tummy.

What is this thing that's stuck up my nose? I wonder what it does. It doesn't really hurt, but it feels kinda funny. Wait, my tummy is gurgling. But it's not because it's hungry. I think it's filling up with milk! But how? It must be some sort of magic.

A short while later, Kat and the puppy were back at home. The puppy was fast asleep in her bubble as she breathed in the little puffs of oxygen.

"Phew!" Kat said as she and Devin sat down on the couch to rest. "I'm glad we have her breathing and eating. Hopefully, she'll gain some strength now."

She was really pleased that the feeding tube was working.

"So how long do you think we'll keep her?" Devin asked.

Most of the time when they took in animals, Kat and Devin kept them until they were healthy enough to go to a foster or to a forever home. In most cases, that took about six to ten weeks.

Kat shrugged. "I have no idea with this one. She seems completely dependent on the oxygen. It might be longer than usual. She's our little bubble baby!"

Then Kat's gaze turned serious. "I feel so bad for her," she told Devin. "I can't even go in there and love on her. And it sure looks like she could use some love. It may be days before she can come out of the bubble."

Kat walked over to the clear plastic enclosure and knelt down. "I love you, little one. Can you feel it?"

And as if she had heard Kat, the puppy opened one eye. And Kat swore she saw the tiniest wag of the puppy's tail.

CHAPTER 4
FINDING A HOME

FOUR DAYS LATER, THE PUPPY WAS still in the bubble, and she was keeping Kat *very* busy. Every two hours, Kat or Devin fed the puppy through the feeding tube. And after each feeding, the puppy looked up at Kat with her chocolate-brown eyes as if she was saying, *"Thank you for taking care of me!"*

Kat felt so much love for the puppy. She wished desperately that she could scoop her up and hold and cuddle her. But the puppy looked so tired, and Kat knew that her lungs weren't fully healed yet. So Kat didn't dare take her out of the bubble.

Kat wanted to keep the Bottle Brigade's followers updated on her new rescue, so she posted a photo of the puppy on Instagram: *A long-haired dachshund brought into the vet after swallowing her milk wrong while nursing . . . We need her lungs to rest up and heal so she can live a wonderful life.*

Immediately, the comments came pouring in:

Stay strong . . . There is so much for you to discover and enjoy.

You are angels . . . Please let us know how the little fur baby gets on.

Kat smiled as she scrolled through the comments. It meant so much to have so many people rooting for her animals. She looked over to the puppy in the bubble: "Everyone's pulling for you. You just hang in there, you hear me?"

I'm so scared and lonely, the puppy thought. *The nice lady that the nice man calls Kat does come to visit. And afterward, my tummy feels full. But I have no one to cuddle with, although the blankets inside here are supersoft.*

Oh, hello, Kat, the puppy thought as Kat approached the bubble. *Is today the day we can cuddle?*

The puppy's spirits started to rise.

"Look at you," Kat said as she peered into the bubble. "Your tail is wagging. Are you feeling better?"

Kat looked at Devin. "I think I'm going to try to take her out again."

Devin nodded. "We've had her on oxygen for a week now. Maybe her lungs are strong enough for her to be out for a little while."

Kat gave her husband a hopeful look and opened the bubble.

But as soon as she took the puppy out, the tiny animal began to gasp for air!

"Too soon," Kat said sadly as she placed the puppy back inside her bubble. "I don't know what else to do for her."

Devin gave his wife a hug. "You know that we're doing everything we can. The only thing we can do now is keep her in the bubble and hope her lungs get stronger."

"But we can't keep her in there forever, can

we?" Kat asked. "I mean, what kind of life would that be?"

Kat's eyes filled with tears. She had never had a puppy inside a bubble for longer than two weeks. And it sure didn't look like this puppy would be able to breathe outside the bubble anytime soon. Would this puppy *ever* be able to live a full life? Or would she be the bubble puppy forever?

Not wanting the puppy to feel any lonelier than she probably already felt, Kat carried the bubble with her wherever she went in the house. Luckily, the bubble was light and easy to transport. And the puppy inside was still so tiny that she really didn't add much weight.

The puppy watched Kat as she cooked and washed dishes in the sink.

The puppy watched Kat as she brushed her teeth first thing in the morning and again at night.

The puppy watched Kat as she played with Etta and her other two dogs, Rylee and Kane.

The outside world looks like so much fun! The puppy thought. *I'm going to work on getting stronger and stronger so I can go out there and play!*

To make the puppy feel more comfortable, each day Kat added another toy or blanket to the bubble: a little white lamb, a pink fluffy blanket, and more.

And as the puppy grew, she became more playful. She licked the wall of the oxygen bubble and nuzzled her toys happily.

She even became a bit mischievous, biting her feeding tube: "You're a bad girl," Kat teased gently.

"So do you think we'll be keeping her forever?" Devin asked Kat the next week. They had now had the bubble puppy for two weeks.

Kat shook her head. "I know we can't. Our job is to get her well enough so that she can be adopted. But I'm falling in love with her."

"I know you are, Kat," Devin said. "But we have three dogs of our own, and as much as I know you'd like to, we can't take on another one."

Kat nodded. "I know," she agreed. "And I don't think we'll have trouble finding this one a home. Even though she's still inside the bubble, she's getting stronger every day. I really think she's going to make it."

"I think so, too," Devin said. "I know there's hope for this little one."

Suddenly, Kat broke out in a huge smile.

"And I just thought of the perfect person to adopt her," Kat said brightly. "Bonnie!"

"Of course!" Devin said. "That would be a great fit."

Bonnie Acosta-Schmeisser was a vet tech supervisor at the same animal hospital where Kat worked. Not only did Bonnie love animals, but she also had a soft spot for dachshunds. In fact, she already had four of her own!

Ginger was rescued from the streets and wasn't a purebred dachshund. Her ears stood straight up, which was a clue that she might have been mixed with a chihuahua. The other three dogs were purebreds: Bella, a dapple smooth-haired dachshund; Zero, a wire-haired dachshund; and Jack, a black-and-tan short-haired dachshund.

Quickly, Kat pulled out her phone and texted Bonnie a photo of the puppy.

Bonnie responded with a ton of hearts. It was love at first sight!

"So, you'll take her?" Kat texted.

"I'd love to," Bonnie responded. "But I have to check with my husband first."

Kat hoped he would say yes.

CHAPTER 5

THE BUBBLE PUPPY GETS A NAME

A FEW MINUTES LATER, KAT'S CELL phone rang.

"It's Bonnie," she told Devin as she glanced down to see who was calling.

"That was quick," Devin said.

"Which could be good news or bad news," Kat said. "Either Bonnie's husband said yes right away, or it's a no."

"Well, if you don't answer your phone right now, you'll never know!" Devin said with a grin.

"Hey, Bonnie," Kat answered the phone, her heart pounding. What would she do if Bonnie turned down this puppy? Sure, she could always find another home, but Bonnie's home would be *perfect*! Plus, she already had four other rescued dachshunds. They would be great friends for this sweet little pup.

"He said yes!" Bonnie shouted into the phone.

Kat breathed out a big sigh of relief and gave Devin a thumbs-up.

Devin pumped his fist in the air.

"When do you think I can take her home?" Bonnie wanted to know.

Kat looked over at the little puppy in

the bubble. While she wasn't struggling to breathe, she wasn't exactly ready yet to live outside the oxygen chamber.

"I'd say another two weeks," Kat told Bonnie. "I can't imagine her being in there longer than that."

"Perfect!" Bonnie said. "We are all *so* excited!"

"Well, that's a relief," Kat said as she ended the call with Bonnie.

Devin nodded in agreement.

The next day, Kat had a surprise in store for the little puppy: She was taking her to work!

"We're going on an adventure today," Kat said as she loaded the bubble puppy into her car. "You are going to make some new friends for sure!"

Kat left for work a bit earlier than usual because she had another surprise up her sleeve.

She pulled up to the hospital, took the chamber out of her car, and rushed inside.

"Surprise!" Kat called, walking into Bonnie's office. Bonnie worked the opposite shift from Kat—from 5 a.m. to 5 p.m.—so she was just getting ready to go home.

"Is that her?" Bonnie asked, dropping her bag on her desk and racing over to Kat.

Kat smiled.

"She is so tiny!" Bonnie said. "And so cute. Hello, Sally."

"I see you already have a name for her," Kat noted.

Bonnie nodded. "Since we already have a Zero and Jack at home, the kids and I thought we should add a Sally to the dachs-hund pack!"

Kat knew what Bonnie was talking about. Zero and Jack were both characters from the movie *The Nightmare Before Christmas*, and so was Sally.

"That's a perfect name for her," Kat told Bonnie. "Just like Sally the rag doll in the movie, this Sally is pretty and shy."

Bonnie laughed. "But I can tell by the twinkle in her eye that she's not going to be shy for long!"

Bonnie picked up her bag and walked to the door. "Goodbye for now, Sally. I can't wait to welcome you to my home in a few weeks."

Kat said goodbye to Bonnie and sat down at her desk. Then she felt a little tug on her heart.

What was it? Was she sad that she would have to let Sally go? Perhaps. But Kat had let go of lots of animals who she had fallen in love with in the past. Still, something about Sally was making it extra hard to think about parting with her.

Sighing, Kat pulled her long hair into a bun and got to work.

"Do you want to come with me as I check on some of our patients?" she asked Sally.

Sally wagged her tail.

"I'll take that as a yes," Kat said with a giggle.

Kat helped care for many animals at the hospital where she worked. Since this was an emergency hospital, Kat saw animals that had been in accidents, had trouble breathing, had swallowed something they shouldn't have, and more. Kat loved that the hospital never closed—it was open twenty-four hours a day, seven days a week. That meant the staff there could try to help animals in need at any time of the day.

Beep! Beep!

Sally turned her head, trying to figure out where the noise was coming from. *I think I've been here before*, Sally thought. *Or at least someplace like it. And it wasn't very fun. I know: It was the place where I couldn't breathe. I mean, I really, really couldn't breathe. I didn't like it there. And I don't like it here now! Kat, can we please go home now?*

When Kat finished changing the bandage on a kitten's paw, she went to check on Sally.

"What's wrong?" Kat asked. Sally was cowering in the corner of her bubble. "You don't like it here, huh? Well, this is a *good* place. A place where we help hurt and sick animals like you. Don't worry, Sally. You're okay here."

Sally looked into Kat's kind eyes and knew she was safe. Still, she wanted to get out of there as fast as she could. But Kat's shift was twelve hours long, so Sally had no choice but to wait.

At last, it was time to go home. But just as Kat was taking Sally and her bubble outside, Bonnie rushed in.

"Phew! I'm glad I didn't miss you. I just had to get another look at adorable Sally!" Bonnie said breathlessly.

Kat laughed. "She is *so* cute, right?"

Bonnie nodded enthusiastically. "I told the kids all about her. They just can't wait to meet her. I hope the next couple of weeks fly by, and that she's healthy enough to come home with me soon."

"She seems to be getting stronger every day," Kat said. "So, fingers crossed!"

Bonnie said goodbye to Sally and Kat. And then Kat and Sally, the little bubble puppy, headed home.

"Sally and I are back!" Kat called out as she walked into her house. It was early, but Devin was awake, taking care of their Bottle Brigade babies.

Devin came to greet Kat at the door. "So, someone finally has a name."

Kat nodded. "We saw Bonnie at the start

of my shift, and she told me she and her family picked Sally for her name."

Devin thought for a moment, and then said, "Oh, I get it. To match their other pets' names from *The Nightmare Before Christmas*."

"Exactly," Kat said.

"You must be exhausted," Kat told Devin. "Just let me get changed and then I'll go to the nursery. Can you take Sally in there and give her some food?"

"Sure thing," Devin said. He prepared the food for Sally's feeding tube.

Even though Kat had been up all night at the hospital, she knew that Devin had been awake with their animals as well. And as soon as Kat fed the animals, she'd be able to take a nap.

Kat went into her bedroom and changed

into some comfortable clothing. Then she washed her face and brushed her teeth. Just as she was about to go back downstairs, she heard Devin's panicked voice.

"Kat, come quick," he called out. "Sally isn't breathing!"

CHAPTER 6

A SETBACK

KAT RACED INTO THE NURSERY.
"What happened?"

"I have no idea," Devin said. "I was just checking on Sally and I saw that she was blue!"

Kat raced over to the oxygen tank. Was it working? She checked to be sure the connection from the oxygen to Sally's bubble was okay. It was. So what could be wrong?

"I'm going to increase the oxygen flow," Kat said, and she turned a knob on the oxygen supply tank.

But after a few minutes, Sally's color hadn't changed. The little puppy was still gasping for air.

Kat grabbed her car keys.

"I'm taking her to the hospital," she said. "Maybe there's something blocking her airway, and that's why she can't breathe."

"Here, take this," Devin held out the portable oxygen.

Since Kat was taking the bubble with her, she had to disconnect from the oxygen tank she had at home. Instead, Kat opened the bubble and fit the tiny oxygen mask over Sally's snout. Then she rushed the little bubble puppy into her car. "Don't worry, Sally, I'm going to get you help."

As soon as the oxygen mask started pumping air, Sally began to breathe a little easier. But she was still blue. And Kat knew this was not good at all.

What is this thing over my nose? Sally thought. *Where are my little puffs of air? Why can't I breathe them in?*

Help me, Kat.

Please help me.

Finally, Kat and Sally arrived at the emergency room.

"I need some help here!" Kat called out.

Of course, everyone there knew Kat, and another vet tech came running over.

Kat quickly explained that Sally had stopped breathing, and that she didn't know why.

"She seems to be breathing a bit now," Kat said, "but she's still blue."

The vet tech brought Kat and Sally into an examining room so Sally could be seen by one of the veterinarians.

I hear those beeping sounds again, just like last time, Sally thought. *And now I can't breathe. Kat, what's happening? Please help me.*

"I don't see anything blocking her airway," the vet, Dr. Garcia, told Kat after a quick examination.

Sally was still struggling to breathe, and her color was not improving. It broke Kat's heart to see the little puppy wriggling and squirming, desperate to take in a drop of air.

"So, what do you think is wrong?" Kat asked.

The vet shook her head. "I'm not sure. But since she's still not getting in enough oxygen, I think we should intubate her."

Kat knew that Dr. Garcia wanted to slide a tube down Sally's mouth and into her windpipe. The tube would keep her windpipe open so oxygen could get to her lungs.

But Kat also knew that once the tube was put down Sally's windpipe, there was a good chance she would become dependent on it. That's because Sally's lungs wouldn't have to work as hard to get oxygen while the breathing tube was in place. Sally's lungs might not develop as they should. And hardworking lungs were what Sally needed to lead a full life.

"I don't want to do that," Kat said firmly. "I don't want her to rely on the breathing tube. What if we just gave her some medicine to calm her down?"

"It's worth a shot," Dr. Garcia said, and she gave Sally an injection.

Within minutes, Sally had settled down. She was breathing a bit more easily.

"I'm glad she's breathing better now," the vet said. "But I'm still very concerned about her."

Kat nodded. "Me too."

"I'm worried there might be something more going on other than just pneumonia," Dr. Garcia said.

"What do you think it could be?" Kat asked.

"She might have been born with some sort of birth defect," the vet explained.

Kat looked worried.

"I'm going to reach out to a specialist," Dr. Garcia told her. "She'll call you when she can fit Sally in."

Just then, Bonnie came running into the examination room. "My Sally!" she shouted. Even though Bonnie was in the middle of her shift, as soon as she heard that Sally was there, she rushed in to see what was going on.

Kat filled her in on what had happened.

"That was a good call to give her the medication instead of intubating her," Bonnie said. "But I'm worried that Dr. Garcia said there could be a birth defect."

Kat nodded. "Me too. If you don't mind,

I'm going to spend the rest of the night here with Sally. I want to be by her side in case she gets worse."

Bonnie gave Kat a big hug. "You're such a good mama. But text me if something happens—good or bad."

Kat promised she would.

Kat sat down next to Sally's bubble. "Oh, little one," Kat said. "You've been through so much in your short time here. You're probably not much more than a month old. But you're a fighter, I just know it."

Sally peeped open an eye and looked at Kat. *Thank you for staying with me, Kat. Thank you for saving me, and for helping me. I love you so much. And I'm going to keep on fighting. You'll see.*

CHAPTER 7
STEP-BY-STEP

THE NEXT MORNING, KAT WOKE UP with a start. At first, she didn't know where she was. But when she heard loud beeping noises and the sounds of animals all around her, she remembered she was at the animal hospital.

She sat up and shook off the blanket that someone had placed over her during the night.

Then her eyes shot over to Sally. Her tiny tongue was pink again!

Kat texted Bonnie: *Good news: Sally's breathing has improved. And her color is looking good!*

Within seconds, Bonnie texted her reply: *I know. I went in and checked on her in the middle of the night. Both of you were sleeping and breathing soundly!*

Thanks for the blanket, lol, Kat replied.

Anything for my best girls, Bonnie texted back.

Kat looked at Sally. Not only was she pink, but she was wagging her tail.

"Okay, my little fighter," Kat said. "Are you ready to go home?"

Sally wagged her tail even faster and Kat laughed.

Kat texted Devin to tell him they were headed home. Then she picked up the bubble (with Sally inside!) and went to the discharge desk.

"You have one strong little puppy there," the nurse said, giving Kat some papers to sign.

Kat nodded. "Yes, I know."

She signed the papers, put Sally into the car, and half an hour later they were home again.

"Welcome back," Devin said as soon as Kat walked through the door with Sally. "Did you manage to get any sleep?"

Kat nodded. "Some. But I'm sure you're tired, too. Why don't you go lie down?"

Devin kissed his wife and headed off to bed.

"Okay, Sally," Kat said once the puppy and her bubble were settled back in the nursery. "You have to rest up, too. And then once you're strong enough, you really have to exercise those little lungs."

Kat didn't want to speak the words out loud about visiting a specialist. But she anxiously awaited her call.

Sally looked at Kat with her brown eyes. *Thank you for taking such good care of me. I love you so much! I'm going to be a good girl and rest and get better. Inside, I'm very strong. Now I just have to prove it to you!*

A few days later, Kat noticed that Sally was pawing at the window of her bubble. "What do you want, baby? Do you want to come out to play?"

Kat and Devin exchanged looks. Was it time to let Sally out again?

Kat wasn't sure. She didn't want to put Sally in any danger. What if the vet was right and Sally did have a birth defect? But, on the other hand, Kat knew Sally had to learn to breathe outside the bubble.

"I'm not so sure about letting her out," Devin said as if reading Kat's mind.

"That's just what I was thinking. Is it too soon after her trip to the emergency room? I haven't heard from the specialist yet. Do you think I should wait until after her appointment? What if there's something else wrong with her?"

Devin thought for a moment. "I think we should let Sally take the lead on this one. I don't think any real harm will come to her by letting her out."

After a few more minutes of pawing, Kat

gave in and unzipped the bubble to see what Sally would do. And the little puppy walked right out!

Oh wow! There is something outside my bubble! Sally thought as she padded along the hardwood floor. *My feet are slipping and sliding. Hey, this is fun! But wait a minute: I'm having trouble breathing again. Help!*

Seeing that Sally was in distress, Kat quickly scooped her up and put her back inside the bubble.

"What a good girl," Kat said. "You were outside your bubble for fifteen seconds!"

As if in response to Kat's praise, Sally wagged her tail.

Even though Sally had a hard time

breathing outside the bubble, it didn't stop her from trying to get out.

"Let's try this again," Kat said the next time she saw Sally pawing at the plastic sides of her enclosure.

Kat unzipped the bubble and Sally hopped out. This time she was outside for thirty seconds. Kat was very happy with Sally's progress.

Each day, Kat let Sally out of the bubble so she could walk around the floor and exercise her lungs a bit. And each time, usually within a minute, she was gasping for air and had to be placed back inside her enclosure.

Kat praised Sally after each venture out of the bubble. "Was it good?" she asked, putting Sally on a fluffy pink blanket, and then zipping up the plastic side.

And Sally would always wag her tail.

"Look who's here," Kat said to Sally as she brought her into her office at the animal hospital. "It's your future mama."

Bonnie rushed over to Sally. "Thanks for getting here a little early so I could see her," Bonnie told Kat. "My, she's grown a lot!"

Kat nodded. "And I really do think her lungs are getting stronger."

Then she turned toward Sally. "Yesterday you stayed out of the bubble for almost forty-five seconds, didn't you, girl?"

"Wow," Bonnie said, impressed. "So, when do you think I can bring her home?"

Kat shook her head. "I really don't know. Things are progressing, but it's been very slow. I've never had a puppy inside a bubble for this long before."

Bonnie put her arm around Kat's shoulders. "I know you're doing your best. And I know you'd never let an animal go to their forever home until they're healthy and stable."

"I know you understand," Kat said. "But I just have so much love for Sally. I want her to get well fast. And there's still the issue of the possible birth defect. I don't have an appointment with the specialist yet."

"I'm sure the specialist will get in touch soon," Bonnie told Kat. "And in the meantime, you just continue doing what you do best: taking care of Sally and showing her lots of love."

Kat nodded, wiping a tear from her eye.

"Well, I've got to get home," Bonnie told Kat. "I have to make the kids dinner."

"And then maybe you can get some rest," Kat said with a laugh. She knew Bonnie probably got just as little sleep as she and Devin!

"We'll see," Bonnie said. "We'll see."

Just then, a nurse ran into Kat's office. "Kat, we need you in the emergency room," she said.

"Gotta run," Kat told Bonnie. Then she picked up Sally's bubble and rushed to the ER. "Let's see who we can help today, Sally," Kat told the little puppy.

Sally's eyes darted around the emergency room. Vets, vet techs, nurses, and assistants hurried back and forth. Since she had been going with Kat to work a lot, Sally was used to all the hustle and bustle. And the beeping noises didn't bother her anymore.

As Sally watched Kat work, her little heart swelled with joy. Sally was just as proud of Kat as Kat was of Sally!

Kat put the ends of her stethoscope in her

ears and listened to a tiny kitten's heartbeat. Then she wrote down something on a piece of paper. And when the veterinarian walked over, Kat told her what she had noted so far about the kitten.

Sally watched as Kat treated patients all day. Well, she didn't exactly watch *everything* Kat did, because a lot of the time Sally was napping!

When Kat and Sally got home, Kat said, "Today, I have exciting news for Sally."

Devin looked up from feeding Hammy. "Really?" he asked. "What is it?"

"I'm going to remove her feeding tube," Kat explained happily. "Since Sally has grown, I had a feeling that her feeding tube didn't reach her stomach anymore. So, when I had a free moment at the hospital, I did an X-ray. And I was right. Today, she'll graduate to puppy food!"

"That's amazing!" Devin exclaimed.

Kat unzipped the bubble and lifted Sally out. "This won't hurt a bit," she told the puppy as she carefully removed the tape from the part of the feeding tube that was attached to her head.

Then Kat gently tugged the tube and it slipped out of Sally's nose.

Sally gave a little cough and a wheeze, and Kat put her back inside the bubble.

After catching her breath, Sally shook her head around a few times, and then rolled happily on a fuzzy blanket.

"Looks like she's glad to be free of that tube," Devin observed.

"And she'll be happy with this, too." Kat slid a little bowl of puppy gruel inside the bubble. The puppy gruel was made by mixing puppy food with puppy formula until it was soft enough for Sally to swallow it easily.

Kat and Devin watched as Sally sniffed the gruel.

"She doesn't know what to make of it," Kat said with a giggle.

Sally walked around the bowl. Then she sniffed the food again.

Finally, Sally lowered her head and opened her mouth.

"Look, she's eating!" Devin exclaimed.

"That's a good girl," Kat said joyfully. "You just take it nice and slow. Take it step-by-step and you'll be strong and healthy in no time!"

CHAPTER 8
BATH AND BUBBLES

"LOOK AT YOU, GOBBLING UP YOUR puppy gruel!" Kat said with a laugh. "And you're getting it all over your cute little face. I think it's time for a bath."

Sally's ears perked up and she looked at Kat. But she really didn't know what was in store for her.

"Devin!" Kat called into the other room. "I want to give Sally a bath. She's getting a bit stinky."

Devin walked into the nursey with a big smile on his face. "I love baths, but I'm not sure Sally will!"

"Okay, I'll be right back," Kat told her husband.

Kat filled the kitchen sink with water, careful to make sure it wasn't too hot or too cold. As soon as the water was the perfect temperature and level, Kat returned to the nursery.

"Now here's the tricky part," Kat explained to Devin. "You're going to have to hold the portable oxygen to Sally's nose while I scrub her clean."

Devin nodded, picked up the portable oxygen, and turned it on.

At the same time, Kat lifted Sally

from her bubble and smiled at the little pup.

"Ready for a little adventure?" Kat asked.

Quickly, Kat and Devin walked to the sink. Devin was careful to keep the oxygen close to Sally's snout so she could breathe.

"One, two, three," Kat lowered Sally into the water.

But Sally didn't like it—not one bit!

What in the world is going on here? Why are Kat and Devin putting me into this giant water bowl? Am I supposed to lap it up? I don't think so. And what is this bubbly stuff that Kat is rubbing over my body? Devin, I need more puffs of air!

The more Sally wriggled, the harder it was for Devin to keep the oxygen over her nose and mouth.

"Try to stay still, little one," Kat urged as she rinsed the soap off Sally's tiny body. "Just a few more minutes and you'll be done!"

When Kat was pretty sure that Sally was clean, she scooped her out of the water and wrapped her in a cozy clean towel. Then she and Devin rushed her back to her bubble.

As soon as Sally was safely back inside the plastic enclosure, she snuggled up next to her favorite teddy bear.

"She's looking at me with such serious eyes," Kat said. "But at least she's clean!"

And then the clean little puppy settled down for a nice, long nap.

"Why the sad face?" Devin asked Kat later that day. "I think Sally's first bath was a success."

Kat shook her head. "It's not that. I'm just

so bummed that Sally's breathing hasn't gotten any better. I mean, she can't stay out of the bubble for longer than a minute or two. What kind of life is that?"

Devin nodded. "I'm sad about that, too. But at least she's eating and growing."

"That's another problem," Kat said.

Devin gave his wife a confused look.

"She's outgrowing her bubble," Kat explained. "I don't know how much longer we can keep her in the one we have for her. With her getting bigger each day, there isn't much room for her to run around."

The two sat in silence for a while, thinking about what to do.

Then Kat had an idea: "I know! I'll build her a bigger bubble! It will be large enough for her to run around inside!"

"But how?" Devin asked. "And with what?"

Kat looked around the nursery. Then she spotted a plexiglass kennel. Plexiglass is a clear material that's very hard to break.

"I think we can build out our plexiglass kennel for her," Kat said.

She went over to the kennel and took a large sheet of plastic and taped it over the top. Then she poked a small hole in the plastic and fed in the oxygen tube.

"Wow!" Devin exclaimed when Kat was finished. "Very creative! This enclosure is three times as big as her old one. I think even I could lie down in it and take a nap!"

Kat smiled. She opened the kennel door and lay down some wee-wee pads (so Sally could pee and poop) and placed her comfy toys and blankets in a corner.

Next, Kat turned on the oxygen and ran her hands around the kennel. Wherever she felt an oxygen leak, she covered that space with blue tape.

"*Voila!*" Kat said when the chamber was secured.

She lifted Sally from her old bubble and placed her in the new one. "Welcome to your new, improved home!"

Sally wiggled her tail. She sniffed the plexiglass walls. Then she trotted over to her toys and began licking them.

"See, Sally," Kat said. "It's a new place, but it has all your friends inside."

Sally looked up at Kat and wagged her tail.

Then she started to run.

"You go, girl!" Devin shouted.

Kat laughed. "I've never seen her run around so much before."

"This is going to be great for her," Devin agreed. "Now she can exercise her lungs *inside* the bubble."

"And there's something even better," Kat said.

"What's that?" Devin wanted to know.

"There's room for visitors!"

And with that, Kat opened the door to the bubble and crawled inside.

Hello, Kat, Sally thought. *Welcome to my new home. This is my feeding area. This is my bathroom. This is my playroom. And this is my bed. What do you want to do first?*

Kat laughed as Sally romped around the bubble. The little puppy played with her toys and scurried over Kat's lap. And as soon as she had had enough playtime, Sally plopped down on a comfy blanket and fell fast asleep.

Quietly, Kat crept out of the bubble.

"Sweet dreams, little one," she whispered softly. "Sweet dreams."

CHAPTER 9
T-SHIRTS AND TROUBLE

"I'M HOME!" KAT CALLED OUT AS she walked in her front door. She had just finished her twelve-hour shift at the hospital and she was exhausted. But Kat knew she had a lot of work ahead of her at home.

Besides caring for Sally, Kat and Devin were constantly taking in other very sick puppies.

"How's Pot Roast doing?" Kat asked as she walked into the nursery.

Like Sally, Pot Roast had pneumonia and was struggling to breathe.

"Not much change," Devin told Kat.

Kat knelt down to get a closer look at the little brown Frenchie inside the oxygen chamber. "You are the fattest potato I've ever seen!" she said affectionately. "Now you work on strengthening your lungs, just like Sally!"

"And speaking about lungs, how's little Sally doing?" Kat asked Devin.

"She seems really happy inside her bubble," Devin said. "She's running and playing with her toys. But . . ."

He trailed off.

"I know," Kat said. "She still can't stay out of the bubble for very long."

Devin nodded sadly.

"I just don't know what we're going to do with her," Kat said with a yawn.

"I don't know, either," Devin said. "But I know what we're going to do with you right now. You're going to lie down and get some rest. I'm sure you had a busy day at the hospital."

Kat nodded and headed off to bed.

When Kat woke up a few hours later, a surprise greeted her: A large box had arrived.

"Ooh, I think I know what this is!" Kat said. She grabbed a pair of scissors and used them to open the box. Once she peeked inside, a huge smile brightened Kat's face.

"They're here!" she shouted as she pulled out a gray T-shirt.

Devin came into the room to see what the commotion was all about. He quickly spotted the T-shirt Kat was holding.

"It looks so great!" he said.

The shirt had a photo of Sally on the front with the words *Just Breathe* right below her adorable face. Besides the gray shirts, there were brown T-shirts and long-sleeved black sweatshirts with the same designs.

"I've got to post these!" Kat said.

Kat quickly snapped photos of the shirts and posted them on The Bottle Brigade's Instagram account.

Sally shirts are up! Kat wrote. *All proceeds go to her medical care.*

Caring for animals in need like Sally is very expensive, and Kat and Devin relied on contributions from their followers. Selling T-shirts was a great way to make money, and the funds helped them purchase medical supplies for all the animals.

As soon as Kat posted photos of the shirts, comments came pouring in.

Omg what a great idea! Just bought one. We're rooting for you, Sally! Xoxo, one follower wrote.

Kat smiled as she scrolled through the comments. There was just so much love out there for Sally!

Just then, Kat's phone rang.

"Hello?" she answered, thinking it was probably a call asking her to take in another animal.

But instead, it was the specialist. She told Kat she could see Sally that day.

"Devin, I'm going to take Sally to the vet," Kat said. "The specialist just called, and she has a last-minute opening."

Kat pulled up in front of the specialist's office, her stomach filled with butterflies. As she lifted Sally and her bubble out of the car and carried them toward the office door, Kat wondered what would happen next. Would the specialist be able to help Sally?

"Well, aren't you a little cutie," the vet said as Kat brought Sally into her office. "I'm Doctor Jill Manion. It's nice to meet you."

Kat smiled and held out her hand to greet the doctor. "Sally is the best little baby," she said. "I just want to find out what's wrong with her so I can help her recover and live her best life. She's been in oxygen for a little over four weeks now. And she can only be out of her bubble for short periods of time."

Dr. Manion examined Sally and then

turned to Kat, a serious look on her face. She explained that Sally might have a condition in which her nerves don't communicate with her muscles. The vet told Kat that might explain why Sally becomes weak after she's been out of the bubble for more than a few minutes.

"I'll do a blood test to see if that's what's going on," Dr. Manion told Kat. "We should have the results in a few days."

The vet explained that there was another possibility as well. She acknowledged that Sally might have been born with a birth defect that affects her lungs. If that was the case, the problem was more serious and might even be life-threatening.

Upon hearing this news, Kat began to cry.

As a vet tech, Kat knew that a microscope had to be lowered into Sally's windpipe to check for signs of a birth defect. And she also knew the doctor wouldn't be able to perform the test yet because Sally's windpipe was still too small.

Dr. Manion placed her hand on Kat's shoulder. "Try not to worry too much right now," she said gently. "Let's just wait and see the results of the blood test."

Kat thanked her, picked up Sally's bubble, and headed back to her car.

Once she got home, Kat told Devin what Dr. Manion had said. He was upset at the news, too, but he tried to lift Kat's spirits.

"You're taking such good care of her, Kat," he said soothingly. "I'm sure Sally can feel all your love."

Kat managed a smile.

"I'm going to post an update on Insta," she said, grabbing her phone. "We can use all the extra support we can get!"

Kat filled in The Bottle Brigade's followers with the details of the visit with the specialist. Then she added a little more about how she was feeling: *I'm dreading the results of the test. I want Sally to live a full, happy life with her family. She doesn't deserve any long-term medical conditions.*

Kat went on to thank her community for their donations to Sally's medical fund. Then she asked everyone to continue to keep Sally in their thoughts.

CHAPTER 10
OUT OF THE BUBBLE

KAT PACED BACK AND FORTH IN
the nursery.

"There's nothing more you can do, Kat,"
Devin reminded her gently. "We just have to
wait until Sally's test results come back."

Kat shook her head. "No. I just know there's

something else I can do. We've had her for five weeks now. We've never had a pup on oxygen for so long."

"You're exhausted," Devin said. "Why don't you rest a bit?"

Kat agreed and walked to their bedroom.

I just know I can help her, Kat thought as she lay down on her bed. But she couldn't fall asleep. Thoughts about what to do for Sally raced through her mind.

Sally's okay when she's in her bubble, but she can't stay out of it for long. How can I help strengthen her lungs?

Just then, Kat's phone rang.

It was a call from Dr. Manion! Would she have some good news?

"Hi, doctor," Kat said as she answered the phone.

As Kat listened carefully, a big smile grew on her face. "Thank you so much!"

She ended the call.

"Devin!" Kat called out happily. "Sally's blood test came back negative!"

"Well, that's a huge relief," Devin said.

"But she did say that there is probably some scarring on her lungs from the pneumonia."

"Is there anything we can do about that?"

Kat shook her head. "The best medicine for that is exercise!"

Kat rushed over to Sally's bubble and crawled in. "You're going to be okay," she said as she lifted Sally onto her lap. "Now we just have to work harder to strengthen your lungs."

Kat gave Sally a huge kiss and crawled out of the bubble.

Wait, Kat! Where are you going? I want to play with you! Don't leave me here alone. I want to go out in the world with you. I know you take me places in my bubble, but I want to be outside, breathing real air on my own! Can you help me? Please?

Sally starting pawing at the sides of the bubble.

"Look, Kat," Devin said. "I think Sally wants to come out!"

"Wow, I think you're right," Kat agreed. "I guess it's worth a try."

She opened the bubble and Sally scampered out.

But after just thirty seconds, Sally was gasping for air. Kat quickly scooped her up and put her back inside.

The next day though, Sally stayed out of the bubble for a full minute!

"Was that good?" Kat asked Sally after she was back in her bubble and resting comfortably.

Sally wagged her tail as if saying, "Yes!"

The next week, Sally stayed out for two minutes. Then for three minutes and then for four!

Oh, hello, Etta! Sally ran up to one of Kat's dogs and playfully pawed her nose. *What's the matter? You don't want to play?*

An older dog, Etta clearly wanted to be left alone. She backed away and walked into another room. But that didn't stop Sally.

Oooh! There are lots of toys out here! This one crunches. This one squeaks. And this one rattles. The world is filled with wonderful things. Oooh! I'm running out of breath. Time to return to my bubble!

"Sally is really amazing me," Kat told Devin. "It's like she knows when she can't breathe, and she returns to her bubble on her own."

"She is pretty impressive," Devin agreed.

"Hey, I have an idea," Kat said. "Why don't we try taking Sally outside?"

"Like *really* outside?" Devin asked. "Without her bubble?"

Kat nodded. "She's able to stay outside her bubble for five minutes now. And she's never touched grass before. So, let's give it a try and see what happens! I have a feeling she's going to love it."

Oh my gosh! This is like a whole new world again! But what is this green stuff underneath my paws? It smells fresh, but it feels kinda funny and slippery. I wonder how it tastes. Yuck! This is not as good as my food. In fact, I don't think it's food at all. At least not for me! Now I'm coughing! Kat, my lungs! Help me!

Seeing that Sally was struggling, Kat quickly scooped her up and put her back inside the bubble.

"You were a good girl," Kat told Sally. "You just have to get used to the outdoors, and to breathing air on your own."

Sally cocked her head, and Kat laughed.

"Why don't you take a little rest now, baby."

And that's just what Sally did.

"I think it's time to try Sally on the grass again," Kat said the next day.

"Yeah, let's do it!" Devin agreed.

This time, Sally really seemed to like the grass! She sniffed. She walked. She sniffed some more. (But she didn't eat any!) And then she ran!

"Look at her go!" Kat exclaimed proudly as she watched Sally dart back and forth across the yard. The little puppy seemed happier than ever.

The wind is tickling my nose. And my ears are really flapping as I run. Oh, hello again, Etta. Do you want to race? Come on, slowpoke! I win!

After seven minutes of romping around the yard, Sally decided it was time to go back inside her bubble.

But each day, it seemed as though Sally really didn't want to be in the bubble much anymore. As soon as Devin or Kat came into sight, Sally began to claw at the plexiglass walls.

"It seems like Sally really likes being outside the bubble now," Devin said.

Kat nodded. "And each time, she's out for a longer period. Her lungs are really getting stronger. I think we should just keep the door open a bit and see what she does."

So each day, Sally would stay out of the bubble for more and more time.

After nearly eight weeks, Kat had a realization.

"I think she stays out more than in," Kat told Devin in surprise.

"I think you're right," Devin agreed. He put his arm around Kat, thrilled to see her looking so relieved and happy about Sally's progress.

"Come on, Sally, let's play!" Kat told the little bundle of energy.

Sally ran around and around the room. She even tried to get Etta to play with her, and sometimes Etta would agree. But Etta would always get tired before Sally.

"Come on, Sally, it's time to go back in your bubble," Kat called after the puppy had been out for a particularly long time.

Although Sally's lungs were getting stronger, Kat didn't want her to totally exhaust herself.

But this time, Sally didn't want to go back in.

Kat picked her up and put her back inside the bubble.

But before Kat had a chance to close the door, Sally whipped around and came back out!

Almost all day long, Kat and Devin tried to get Sally to go back into the bubble.

But each time, she refused.

Finally, Kat gave in: "It looks like our little Sally is out of the bubble for good!"

When **SALLY** came to stay with Kat
Mongrain, this tiny dachshund puppy
was just a few weeks old. Kat is a licensed
veterinary technician who helps animals
with special needs, and Sally was having
trouble breathing.

Kat placed Sally in a special plastic bubble full of oxygen. Kat and her husband, Devin, gave Sally lots of love—and cuddly friends and blankets to snuggle with inside her breathing bubble!

Sally was determined to breathe on her own. She practiced by spending small amounts of time outside her bubble.

When Sally outgrew her first bubble, Kat designed a new one that was big enough for visitors!

Slowly but surely, Sally's lungs grew stronger. After many weeks, it was finally time for Sally to step out of her bubble and into the world!

Now that Sally was breathing on her own, she needed a forever home. Kat's friend and coworker Bonnie Acosta-Schmeisser adopted her. Bonnie's other pets are all dachshunds, too!

Sally settled in at Bonnie's house right away. She celebrated her first birthday in style with Bonnie's kids, Emma and Gavin.

Today, Bonnie and her family love to take Sally on new adventures. Sally loves going to the beach.

She also loves going for a swim and eating vanilla ice cream!

This determined, fun-loving pup never gave up on her dream of breathing on her own. To celebrate how far she's come, Sally loves spending time outdoors in the fresh air.

CHAPTER 11
WELCOME HOME

FEBRUARY 27, 2022, WAS BOTH A sad and a happy day for Kat.

It was sad because she had to say goodbye to Sally. And it was happy because Kat knew that Sally was going to the perfect home for her. Plus, Kat was sure she'd still be able to see Sally at work. And Kat knew

Bonnie would keep her updated on Sally's progress.

"Don't forget this." Devin handed a toy lamb to Kat. "It's one of Sally's favorites."

Kat took the toy from Devin and put it into the bag she was packing for Sally.

"Thanks," she told Devin. "I want Sally to have all her favorite toys and blankets at Bonnie's."

Devin laughed. "She's going to be one spoiled puppy," he said, shaking his head. "You just know Bonnie already has a whole load of toys for Sally at her house."

"Well, after all she's been through, she deserves to be treated like a princess," Kat said.

"True," Devin agreed.

"And speaking of princesses," Kat said,

"I think we should deliver Sally to Bonnie sparkling clean."

Devin drew in a deep breath. "Does that mean what I think it does? You know how Sally dislikes baths."

Kat nodded. "Bath time, Sally!" she called.

Sally cocked her little head to one side. *Oh no!* she thought. *Do I hear water? There is no way I'm getting into that big water bowl again.*

And with that, she took off. Sally raced around and around with Kat trying to catch her. Finally Sally got tired, and she plopped down on her dog bed.

Kat quickly scooped her up and placed her in the bath.

"Okay, Sally," Kat said after Sally was clean and dry. "It's time to go."

Kat took a deep breath. She knew she couldn't hold on to Sally any longer. It was time to bring her to her forever home.

"Welcome to your new home, little angel," Bonnie said as Sally ran into her house.

Kat giggled as Sally immediately made herself comfortable.

Hello, Bonnie. This is a nice house. Can I play here? I see a bed! Is that for me? Ohhh! Look at all those toys!

Sally took off to explore her new home.

"I'm so glad she's healthier now," Bonnie told Kat.

"Me too," Kat agreed. "It was a long road, but we made it!"

"You're the best," Bonnie said, giving Kat a big hug.

Kat's eyes began to tear up. "I'm going to miss this little one so much," she said.

"I know you will," Bonnie replied. "You've really established a close attachment to her."

Kat nodded, wiping her eyes.

"But look on the bright side," Bonnie continued. "You can see her at work whenever you want. And you'll always be a part of Sally's family."

Kat knew Bonnie was right. And she was thrilled that Sally now had such an amazing family. Kat knew Sally would get lots of love and attention from Bonnie, her husband, Brian, and their two children, nine-year-old Emma and eight-year-old Gavin. And, of course, her new dog siblings.

"Goodbye, Sally!" Kat called. "See you soon!"

But Sally was too busy exploring her new home to say goodbye to Kat.

What do we have here? Four dogs! Hello, I'm Sally. I'm your new sister! Sally walked over to meet Jack, Zero, Ginger, and Bella. But the dogs just stared at her. *Um, I'm nice. And fun. You'll see! Does this mean I won't be the only dog here? Hmm . . . I don't know what to think about that. And there are also two kids. Fun! Maybe I'll go play with them.*

"Oh my gosh!" Bonnie's daughter, Emma, called out as she rushed over to meet Sally. "She is so, so cute!"

"And so tiny!" Bonnie's son, Gavin, added. He reached down to scoop up Sally.

"Be careful, Gavin," Emma cautioned. "Her back is delicate." Emma knew that since dachshunds have such long bodies, their spines are fragile. And since Sally was still so little, Emma wanted to take extra care.

"I know that, Emma," Gavin said as he gently picked up Sally.

Sally wriggled in Gavin's arms as she licked his face.

Gavin laughed. "I think she likes me!"

Gavin gently blew in Sally's face. "Do you like that?"

But Sally did not like that. Not one bit!

She gave out a yelp and jumped from Gavin's arms.

"Gavin, what did you do?" Emma asked, gently picking up Sally.

"Nothing. I just blew in her face. Softly,"

Gavin said. "The other dogs like that. Sometimes it makes them sneeze!"

"She probably didn't like it because it reminded her of being in oxygen," Bonnie told her son. "She had a lot of oxygen blowing on her when she had trouble breathing."

Gavin nodded. "That makes sense. Sally, I promise never to do that again!"

"I wonder if there's anything else she doesn't like?" Emma asked.

"Baths," Bonnie said. "Kat said she absolutely hates baths!"

"Well, I'm not going to give her a bath right now," Emma said. "I'm going to give her a tour of her new home."

And with that, Emma headed upstairs with Sally snuggled in her arms.

"This is my room. Do you like it?" Emma

said as she placed the puppy on her bed. "And I have a surprise for you."

Emma opened her closet and pulled out a little doggie-sized tutu.

"Now we can be matching," she told Sally as she twirled around in her own tutu.

Gently, Emma put the tutu on Sally. And as soon as she did, Sally was off!

"Hey, where are you going?" Emma asked. "I want to show you Gavin's room next."

But Sally wasn't paying attention to Emma. She was too busy running around in her tutu and exploring her new home.

She sniffed the carpets.

She played with her stuffed animals.

She slid a bit on the wood floor.

Finally, she reached the room Bonnie shared with her husband, Brian. There, she found a soft dog bed just for her and immediately fell asleep!

"Emma! Sally!" Bonnie called out. "Where are you?"

"Shhh, Mom," Emma said. "Sally's sleeping."

Bonnie laughed. "So you tired her out already?"

Emma shook her head. "Nope. She tired herself out. She was running around wildly. She is such a Silly Sally."

"When she wakes up, I think we should take her to the dog park," Bonnie said.

Emma looked concerned. "Are you sure? I mean, she really hasn't been outside much, has she?"

Bonnie shook her head. "No, she hasn't. But I think it's time she learned what it's like to be with other dogs."

"Good afternoon, sleepyhead," Bonnie said as Sally opened her eyes and stretched. "Are you ready to go out?

But unlike Bonnie's other dogs, Sally didn't react to the words *go out*. That was because she had never been taken out on a walk before!

Just then, Emma appeared with a little pink harness and leash. "I want to make sure Sally is leashed up securely for our walk. I don't want to take a chance that she can escape."

Bonnie laughed and gently messed up Emma's brown hair. "I love how cautious you are, Emma."

"And responsible," Emma added, standing up a little straighter.

Securely leashed, Bonnie led Sally outside, followed by Emma and Gavin.

Bonnie got everyone into the car and they drove to the dog park.

"This is going to be a special day for Sally," Bonnie told Emma and Gavin. "But we must be patient with her and follow her lead. If she gets tired and slows down, we'll slow down, too."

Emma and Gavin nodded.

When they arrived at the park, Bonnie went around to the back seat to open the door. Emma popped out first, holding Sally's leash.

"Wait up, Sally!" Emma cried as Sally pulled on her leash and headed straight for the park.

Sniff, sniff, sniff. There are so many new things to smell! There are funny-looking sticks and some green grass. And so many other dogs. I don't want to stop exploring!

Just then, a French bulldog approached Sally. This dog was very friendly and very excited— probably a bit too excited for Sally!

Bonnie laughed as Sally tried to hide behind her legs.

"It's okay, Sally," Bonnie reassured her. "It's just a friendly Frenchie."

But Sally wasn't sure what to make of this little black dog with the turned-up nose who was jumping all over the place. She tugged her leash in the opposite direction.

"I can't believe how long she's been walking," Bonnie said a few minutes later. "It's been at least ten minutes and she hasn't stopped."

"You go, girl!" Gavin shouted, running out in front of Sally.

Seeing Gavin race ahead, Sally raced ahead, too.

"I don't know how you can run so fast with those short little legs," Bonnie said with a laugh. "This has probably been the longest walk you've ever been on!"

"Mom," Gavin put in. "It's the *only* walk she's been on!"

Bonnie laughed.

But Emma was growing concerned. "Mom, do you think we should slow down or stop?"

Bonnie shook her head. "I think Sally knows her limits. She'll let us know when she's had enough."

And that's just what Sally did. After a

while, she sat down in the grass, her tongue hanging out of her mouth.

Bonnie promptly picked her up, and she and the kids went back to the car. Once everyone was buckled into their seats, Sally let out a big yawn.

"Don't worry, Sally," Emma said. "We'll be back at your new home soon. And then you can take a nice, long nap!"

CHAPTER 12

SILLY SALLY

"MOM, COME QUICK!" EMMA CRIED out. "Sally has the toilet paper!"

Bonnie rushed into the living room. Sure enough, Sally held a long strand of toilet paper in her mouth.

"Sally, no!" Bonnie said. But she couldn't help laughing. Sally had grabbed the end of the toilet paper from the roll in the bath-room and was racing around the house with it in her mouth!

"Drop it, Sally!" Bonnie commanded.

But Sally didn't listen. She was having too much fun!

"I guess her true nature is coming out," Bonnie said, finally releasing the toilet paper from Sally's mouth. "You are such a silly girl!"

"Come on, Sally," Emma said. "Time for an outfit change!"

Emma held up a leopard-spotted dress with a pink bow. And, of course, some of the spots were pink, too!

Emma picked up Sally, but she wriggled out of her arms. She wanted to play!

"You can play while wearing your new dress," Emma told her.

Finally, Emma managed to put the dress on Sally.

Whee! Sally thought as she spun around in circles. *I like this dress, Emma! I look so pretty! Wait, do I see spots? Are the spots on me? I think I can get those spots if I just turn faster and faster and faster!*

Emma giggled as Sally spun around and around.

Just then, Gavin walked into the room holding a small blue rubber ball.

"Wanna play soccer?" Gavin asked Sally.

Sally stopped spinning and looked up at Gavin.

Gavin tossed the ball to Sally, who raced after it on her short little legs. When she caught up to the ball, she gave it a little kick.

"She shoots! She scores!" Gavin called.

Just then, Zero and Jack trotted over. They wanted to play, too. But Sally hogged the ball. And she was faster than the other dogs, too.

"Looks like Sally is telling the other dogs that she's the boss!" Gavin said.

"And it looks like Jack and Zero have given up trying to play," Emma added.

After playing with the ball for a little while longer, Sally ran over to her gray fluffy bed that was in the corner of the living room.

Although she was panting, she was still wagging her tail.

"I see you've tired her out," Bonnie said to her children.

"She's just so much fun!" Gavin said.

"And *so* cute!" Emma added.

Bonnie nodded. "Plus, I love how she knows when she's had too much and gives herself a time-out."

Gavin looked puzzled. "A time-out? She didn't do anything naughty."

Bonnie laughed. "That's true. I just mean she knows when she's had enough running around and needs to rest."

"Oh, I get it," Gavin said.

Although Sally was permanently out of the bubble now, her lungs had some scarring on them. Because of the pneumonia, the tissue in Sally's lungs had become thicker, making it harder for her to breathe. Most of the time, she was able to take in enough oxygen, but she still needed to rest. And Sally always knew when it was time to chill out!

After Sally had relaxed for a bit, Bonnie

had an idea: "I think we should take Sally camping!"

"Like, right now?" Emma asked, her eyes wide in surprise.

"No, no," Bonnie said with a laugh. "I mean we should plan a camping trip for the entire family—including Sally!"

"But, Mom, the campground has a lake," Gavin added. "Does Sally know how to swim? And if Sally really doesn't like baths, how will she go swimming with us and the rest of the dogs?"

"Well, I think we should get her used to water," Bonnie suggested. "Right, Sally?"

Sally ran over to Bonnie and started jumping up and down.

"Do you want to go outside?" Bonnie asked.

Sally wagged her tail and barked.

"I'll take that as a yes," Bonnie said.

After a short walk on the leash, Bonnie let Sally out in their backyard. There, Emma and Gavin were sitting in a blow-up pool that had been filled with a little bit of water.

"I guess you two took the 'getting used to water' seriously!" Bonnie noted.

"Mom, put her in!" Gavin urged.

Bonnie picked up Sally. "Okay, but remember, we'll have to let her set her own pace, okay?"

Emma and Gavin nodded in agreement.

Gently, Bonnie set Sally down in the pool.

"Do you want to go swimming?" Bonnie asked. "What do you think?"

Sally didn't know what to think. The pool was much bigger than her sink bathtub. And it didn't have much water in it.

Cautiously, Sally took a step. Then she sniffed the water and took another step.

Why am I in the bath again? But wait, this looks different from my usual bath. And Emma and Gavin are here, too. I don't like my paws in the water. I can lift one up at a time, but I can't lift all of them, because then I'll fall. And my whole body will be in the water. Yuck!

I have to figure out a way out of this. If I walk on the outside of this tub, I won't have to splash in too much water. And now I can jump on Emma's lap. Oh, now I can hop over to Gavin! And then to the edge. And I can jump down to the grass. I'm free!

Even though Sally didn't really like the blow-up pool, the family kept on trying to get her accustomed to the water.

One day, Sally didn't immediately jump out of the pool when she was put in.

"That's a good girl!" Bonnie exclaimed. "Are you ready for a treat?"

At the sound of the word *treat*, Sally's ears perked up. And today, Bonnie had a special surprise in store for Sally!

"Come on Sally," Bonnie said, picking her up and buckling her into her car seat. (Yes, Sally has a car seat!) "We're going to the toy store!"

"Hello, pretty baby," the shopkeeper said as soon as Sally and Bonnie walked into the store. She reached down to pet Sally, but Sally was more interested in exploring.

The shopkeeper pulled down a cute white lamb. *Squeak! Squeak!* went the toy. But Sally just sniffed the lamb and walked away.

Sally stretched her neck and looked at a purple dragon hanging on a hook.

"I see you looking," Bonnie said. She reached up, took down the dragon, and held it out for Sally to sniff. But Sally wasn't interested in that toy, either!

"Do you want to keep looking?" Bonnie asked as Sally led her around the store.

At last, Bonnie found a little brown squeaky hedgehog. She held it out to Sally. She sniffed and sniffed and didn't walk away!

Bonnie took the hedgehog out of its packaging and put it on the ground. Sally nudged the toy with her nose, and it rolled across the ground. Sally liked it!

"Aww, look," Bonnie said. "It's love at first sight."

Bonnie picked up the toy, went to the

register to pay for it, and took Sally and her new toy home.

A few days later, Bonnie and Brian packed up the rest of the family and Sally (and her hedgehog!) for their camping trip. Jack, Zero, Bella, and Ginger were coming along, too.

When they parked their camper at the campground, the first thing Emma and Gavin wanted to do was go swimming.

"Don't forget to put on Sally's life jacket," Bonnie reminded them as they got ready to go to the lake.

"Got it!" Emma said as she fit a tiny bright-yellow-and-blue life jacket on Sally.

And what happened when they put Sally in the lake? She absolutely loved it! She paddled and paddled and didn't want to get out!

As Sally swam in the lake, Bonnie texted Kat to tell her how far Sally had come.

Kat was so thrilled with this news that she posted about Sally's camping trip on The Bottle Brigade's Instagram account:

Look at this girl. She's amazing. She is enjoying life outside the bubble with her new mommy (a friend and vet tech). She's out camping this week with the fam. This makes my heart SO happy.

CHAPTER 13
THE DODO CALLS

BONNIE FELT SOMETHING NUDGE her. She peeped open one eye and looked at the clock.

It was three o'clock in the morning. She had another half hour to sleep before she had to get up for work. Who, or what, was bothering her?

Bonnie rolled over and tried to go back to sleep.

But then she heard a jingling sound. What could it be?

This time, she sat up in bed and rubbed her eyes.

It was Sally, holding her leash. Did she have to go out?

Not wanting to wake up Brian, Bonnie got dressed and took Sally out for a short walk.

"You're up mighty early this morning," Bonnie said with a yawn.

Usually, when Bonnie woke up for her shift, Sally was fast asleep. Bonnie was able to sneak out of the house without disturbing her family or the dogs.

But not today.

"Okay, Sally," Bonnie said in a low voice

when they returned from their walk. "It's time for me to go to work, and time for you to go back to sleep."

Sally just stood there wagging her tail. It certainly didn't look as though she was tired. And then, she ran over to her leash and grabbed it in her mouth.

Bonnie laughed. "Oh, I get it now. You want to come to work with me!"

Sally wagged her tail even harder, as if she understood what Bonnie was saying.

Bonnie leashed Sally up again and headed to her car.

When they arrived at the animal hospital, Kat was more excited than usual when she saw them.

"You're not going to believe this," Kat told Bonnie.

"What happened?" Bonnie asked. "Did you have a record number of emergencies during your shift?"

Kat shook her head.

"No," she said quickly. "I got a call from the Dodo! They want to do a segment on Sally!"

"Oh my goodness!" Bonnie exclaimed. "That is absolutely amazing!"

Bonnie knew that the Dodo posted heartwarming stories about animals. And Bonnie also knew that the Dodo had *tons* of followers. Sally was going to be famous!

"I gave the producer your number, and she's going to give you a call," Kat told Bonnie.

Bonnie started to feel nervous.

"I'm not sure I'll be so good at those interviews," she told Kat. "I mean, you're a natural in front of the camera. Me, not so much."

Kat laughed. "You'll be great!" she said encouragingly. Then she gave Bonnie a big hug.

But Bonnie wasn't so sure. Kat had lots of experience in front of the camera. She posted videos on the Bottle Brigade's Instagram account all the time. Plus, some of her animals had been featured on the Dodo before, including Etta and Hammy.

"I guess I shouldn't really be surprised that you got a call," Bonnie said. "You have posted a lot of adorable pictures and videos about Sally."

Kat nodded. "That's true," she agreed. "And Sally's such a special little pup. I can't wait for the world to fall in love with her."

Bonnie waited until dinner that evening to tell her family the news.

"You're not going to believe what Kat told me today," she announced.

"She has another dachshund puppy for us?" Emma asked.

"Nope," Bonnie said.

"*Two* puppies?" Gavin suggested.

"No more puppies," Bonnie said with a laugh.

"Tell us!" Emma urged.

Bonnie smiled with anticipation. She knew her kids would be *so* excited when they heard the news.

"The Dodo called," Bonnie told them. "They want to do a story on Sally!"

Emma and Gavin leapt up from the table and jumped up and down with joy.

"I can't believe it!" Emma squealed. "Sally's going to be famous!"

"What do you think, Brian?" Bonnie asked her husband.

"As long as you're going to handle it, I'm okay with it," Brian said. "But I'm definitely going to stay off camera!"

"Are they going to bring a crew here to film?" Gavin asked.

Bonnie shrugged. She wanted to say that she hoped not, but she didn't want to disappoint the kids. "I have to wait and see what the producer says when she calls me."

The next day, Bonnie received a call from the producer. They decided that a producer would come over to her house to film over two days.

Upon hanging up, Bonnie called Kat.

"The Dodo is going to come here, and I'm kinda freaking out," Bonnie told her friend.

"You and Sally are going to do great," Kat said.

"It's not Sally I'm worried about," Bonnie said.

Kat laughed. "I know," she said. "But just be yourself and everything will be fine.

On a very hot August day, a Dodo producer rang Bonnie's doorbell.

"He's here!" Emma shouted.

"Hello, I'm Eli," the producer said as he stepped inside.

Sally jumped up to greet him.

"Aren't you adorable?" Eli said, noting Sally's pink tutu.

"And I have lots of costume changes if you need them," Emma added.

Eli laughed. "I'm just going to film as if

you're going through a regular day with Sally."

"Well, a regular day means lots of clothes for her!" Gavin said.

Eli smiled.

"Great," he said. "Let's get started, then."

But Bonnie seemed concerned.

"It's going to be fine," Eli reassured her. "Just go about your day and try to forget I'm here."

"It's just that it's really hot outside," Bonnie pointed out. "I don't want Sally to get overheated."

"I get it," Eli said. "Let's just take some short trips outside. We'll do most of the filming indoors where it's cool."

Bonnie was happy with the plan. And Sally, Emma, and Gavin had lots of fun. They briefly played in the pool in the backyard.

They showed off Sally's toys (and outfits!) Then it was time to go out for a bit longer.

"Let's take Sally to dinner," Bonnie suggested. "We'll go to a dog-friendly restaurant so she can meet other dogs!"

The family and Eli piled into the car and drove about ten minutes to the restaurant.

Sally immediately befriended a large poodle mix. She sniffed her nose. Then she sniffed her butt! Everyone had a great time. And once they were back in the car, Bonnie surprised Sally with a very special treat: a cup of vanilla ice cream!

Sniff! Sniff! Sally stuck her nose into the cup of ice cream. *This stuff is cold and some of it has stuck onto my nose. I have to lick it off. Yum! It's sweet. I want more. Whoa, brain freeze!*

After a long day of filming, the family was exhausted. But Sally still had some energy left. She grabbed a plastic bottle out of the recycling bin and ran around, trying to find someone to play with. But no one wanted to play—not even the other dogs.

The next day, Eli returned for a second day of filming. Since it was still boiling hot outside, most of the filming took place indoors.

Eli asked Bonnie a few questions. She tried her best to answer naturally.

"She was a little angel," Bonnie said about bringing Sally home. "As soon as she got here, I set her up in the living room and introduced her to the other dogs."

"Cut!" Eli called out. "Let's try that again.

"Did I do something?" Bonnie asked.

"No, not at all," Eli said, smiling. "I just want to film you and Sally from different angles."

Relieved that she hadn't done anything wrong, Bonnie began chatting again with the camera rolling.

"How long until Sally's video comes out?" Gavin wanted to know after they were done filming for the day.

"I'm not sure," Bonnie said. "But Eli will let us know."

"Well, I hope it's soon," Gavin said. "Because I can't wait until Sally is introduced to the world!"

CHAPTER 14
A STAR IS BORN

ON SEPTEMBER 17, 2022, BONNIE woke up at 3:30 a.m. to get ready for her shift at the animal hospital. Of course, Sally was awake, too!

Quietly, Bonnie dressed and leashed up Sally. But before she left the house, she wrote a note to her family:

Today's the day! Sally's story will be out in the world! Try not to watch it before our family watch party tonight. xxoo Mom

Bonnie left the note on the kitchen table and walked out the door, with Sally leading the way.

The sun hadn't risen yet, but the temperature was already in the mid-seventies.

"It's going to be another hot one, today, Sally," Bonnie said. "I'm glad we'll be inside most of the day!"

As soon as Bonnie and Sally reached the hospital, Kat was there to greet them.

"It's a big day today!" Kat exclaimed, taking Sally into her arms.

"Yes!" Bonnie agreed. "I can't wait to see the video, but I'm nervous, too."

"I *know* it's going to be great," Kat said encouragingly.

"Thanks," Bonnie told her friend. "I'd invite you over for our family watch party tonight, but I imagine you'll be busy sleeping or taking care of your babies."

"You're right," Kat said, smiling. "I'd love to join, but the animals in need keep on coming in!"

"I don't know how you do it," Bonnie said, her voice full of awe.

Kat laughed. "You do it, too," she teased Bonnie. "Between your work here and your dog and human babies, you're pretty busy yourself!"

Bonnie smiled. "That's true," she agreed. "And we both do it out of love."

The friends said goodbye, and Bonnie got ready for her shift.

"You're finally home!" Gavin burst out impatiently as his mom and Sally walked in the door later that day.

Bonnie ruffled his dark head of hair. "I know you're anxious to watch," she told her son. "I brought home pizza. And as a special treat, we can eat in front of the TV tonight."

Brian had already hooked up the television so the video could play on a larger screen than a computer or phone. The family quickly settled down to watch.

"I brought her into my nursery at home where we have an oxygen bubble," Kat began in the video.

"Look, Sally!" Emma exclaimed. "It's little you. Aww, you were so sick. And tiny."

"Quiet, Emma," Gavin shushed his sister. "I can't hear."

"She was completely oxygen dependent," Kat continued. *"We couldn't take her out of the oxygen chamber at all."*

Bonnie took a bite of pizza and marveled at all the amazing work Kat had done with Sally, even though she already knew the story.

The family watched in silence as Kat's voice told the story of tiny Sally's struggle to take in oxygen. At one point, Bonnie wiped a tear from her eye.

"Don't cry, Mom," Emma whispered. "The story has a happy ending."

"I know," Bonnie whispered back, so as not to disturb the rest of the family. "But my heart bleeds for everything Sally went through."

Emma reached over and squeezed her mom's hand.

"Look, Mom, it's you!" Gavin exclaimed when Bonnie appeared on the screen.

"*Gavin*," Emma said, urging her brother to be quiet.

In the video, Kat explained that she and Bonnie worked together as vet techs in the hospital.

"*From the very beginning, we knew she (Bonnie) was going to adopt her*," Kat explained.

Upon hearing those words, Bonnie picked up Sally. "And I'm so glad I did," she whispered into one of Sally's little floppy ears.

The video continued to show Sally in her new home, playing with Emma and Gavin, trying to get used to the water, and, of course, making some mischief!

Hey, that's me on that big box on the wall! Sally thought as she saw images of herself on the television. *But how can I be up there when I'm down here, too? Oh, I like that toy. And there's my plastic bottle. Wait, I need to play down here, too. And run around in circles. And jump. And run. And wait . . . I'm getting a bit tired now. Time to find my bed.*

Toward the end of video, the family heard Kat's voice again: *"To see her where she is now is the best feeling in the world. And that is why we fight so hard for these babies. And I'm so glad that we did, because now she's a healthy puppy and she gets to live the rest of her life with an amazing family."*

Again, tears rolled down Bonnie's cheeks.

"Are you okay?" Brian asked as the video's final credits rolled.

Bonnie nodded. "These are tears of joy," she explained. "I'm just so happy that Sally is part of our family."

"Me too," Brian agreed.

"And I caught a few glimpses of you on the video, too," Bonnie teased her husband.

Brian blushed.

"Yeah, at least I didn't have a speaking part," he said. "But you were great!"

"Mom! Dad!" Emma called out from in front of the family computer. "Comments about Sally's videos are coming in!"

"Can you read some to us?" Gavin asked.

"There are *tons*, but I'll pick out a few," Emma said. *"This actually teared me up a bit. The world needs more kindness like this."*

"So true," Bonnie said, nodding.

"And this one," Emma continued, reading

another comment. *"Melted my heart when she was wagging her tail when she went back into the bubble. She knew she had to be in there, but you could see that she was happy and resolved to keep trying. What a little champion!"*

After hearing that one, Gavin lifted Sally over his head.

"Sally the bubble puppy," Gavin crowed proudly. "Champion of the world!"

CHAPTER 15
OFF TO THE RACES

"I HAVE SOME EXCITING NEWS," Bonnie told Emma and Gavin a few days later over breakfast.

"After Sally and her video on the Dodo, I don't know how much more excitement I can take," Emma joked.

Bonnie laughed.

"I signed Sally up for the annual Houston Texans Wiener Dog Races!" Bonnie exclaimed.

"Wow, Mom!" Gavin cried. "That's awesome!"

But Emma wasn't so excited.

"What's wrong, honey?" Bonnie asked her daughter, concerned.

"Do you think she can do it?" Emma asked. "I mean, she seems healthy and all, but her lungs are scarred."

"I'm sure she'll be fine," Bonnie said. "Look at how much she runs around at home and outside. It's a short race, and Sally knows her limits. She might even surprise us and win!"

Emma listened quietly to Bonnie. She knew her mom was a vet tech and that she would never endanger Sally.

"Okay," Emma agreed, smiling. "You bet I'll be there to cheer Sally on!"

On October 30, 2022, Bonnie woke filled with anticipation. Today was the day of the Wiener Race! The race was to be held at NRG Stadium in Houston during the halftime show of the Houston Texans and Tennessee Titans football game.

Suddenly, Bonnie shot up in bed and looked around. Where was Sally?

"Sally!" she called out.

But Sally didn't come running.

Quickly, Bonnie dressed and raced downstairs.

"Good morning, sleepyhead," Emma greeted her mom. "We're all ready for the race. How about you?"

Bonnie laughed. Emma was decked out in a cheerleading outfit. And Sally was dressed as a bumblebee!

"You both look adorable," Bonnie said.

"Do you get it, Mom?" Emma asked. "Today, Sally is going to fly as fast as a bee."

"Very cute," Bonnie said. "But you know the game doesn't start until four. And Sally's not racing until halftime. Why are you ready so early?"

"Because I'm too excited to sleep!" Emma said.

"Well, today's my day to sleep in," Bonnie said, ruffling her daughter's hair lovingly. "And *I'm* going back to bed!"

"Don't forget to grab a jacket," Bonnie told her family as they got ready to leave for the stadium.

"But Mom, it's so hot out," Gavin complained.

"Not really," Bonnie told him. "It's supposed to drop into the fifties tonight. And you know it can be chilly in the stadium."

"Okay," Gavin said, grabbing his football jacket.

The family piled into the car, and Bonnie secured Sally in her car seat. "This is a big day for you, little one!"

"And no matter what, you're going to come back a *wiener!*" Gavin joked.

The family cracked up.

"Are we there yet?" Gavin asked after about ten minutes in the car.

Bonnie shook her head. "You know it takes about forty minutes to get to the stadium. And we've only been in the car for ten minutes."

"Which means we have about half an hour left," Emma said.

"Can you hurry up, Mom?" Gavin asked.

"We don't want to get a speeding ticket, Gavin," Brian said. "That would be dangerous."

"Not to mention, irresponsible," Bonnie said. "We're carrying precious cargo!"

A short while later, Bonnie pulled the car into a special parking spot reserved for those participating in the race. The lot was full, and she could hear cheers coming from the stadium.

Brian looked at his phone. "Well, we didn't miss much. There's no score yet."

Just then, the crowd roared.

"I take that back," Brian said. "Houston just scored a field goal."

Gavin pumped his fist and gave his sister a high five. "Yes!" he shouted.

"Come on," Bonnie said. "Let's go. We don't have much time until halftime."

The family hurried through a special entrance, checked in Sally for the race, and received special badges that would allow them to go out onto the field with her.

"This is so exciting!" Emma said, peeking out onto the field. "Oh no! The Titans just scored a touchdown."

The crowd was silent except for a few cheers from the Tennessee fans.

"Now we're losing," a dejected Gavin said.

"Don't worry," Bonnie said. "The wiener races will cheer everyone up!"

"Halftime!" someone shouted to the people waiting to race their dogs. "Now remember, there will be two heats. And the winner of each heat will go head-to-head in the finals."

Brian picked up Sally. She was racing in the first heat and would run toward Bonnie, who was calling her at the finish line. Bonnie's heart started to pound fast. She was so excited for Sally but a little nervous, too. Would Sally know what to do? Would she run in the right direction? Would she freeze?

Carefully, Brian placed Sally behind gate number five. He knelt down and held tight to Sally, who was trying to wriggle free. "You have to wait until they say 'start,'" Brian told a very excited Sally.

Where am I? And why is Brian holding on to me? I just want to run, run, run! This green grass looks like so much fun. Oh look! There's a giant cow over

*there. And there are girls holding pom-poms, just
like the ones Emma has.*

"On your mark, get set, GO!" the announcer
called. "And they're off!"

Whee! Sally thought as she raced down the field.
*Come on, slowpokes. Try to catch me! I bet you can't.
Oh look! There's Bonnie standing at the end. How
did she get there so quickly? I'm coming, Bonnie . . .*

As Sally crossed the finish line, Bonnie scooped
her up into her arms.

The crowd went wild.

"You did it, my little bumblebee!" Bonnie
said proudly. "You came in first!"

"Congratulations, Sally!" the announcer
said. "You are advancing to the finals."

A photographer raced over and snapped Sally's photo.

"Now we just have to wait and see who you'll be racing against," Bonnie said as the second group of dogs got ready to run.

"Looks like you'll be racing against Bug," Bonnie said, pointing to a long-haired dachshund dressed in an adorable pink outfit.

Bonnie had seen Bug race before, and she knew she was fast. She would be tough competition for Sally!

Bonnie jogged down the field and put Sally behind the gate.

"On your mark, get set, GO!" the announcer called out.

Sally and Bug were off!

But Sally's tiny legs couldn't keep up with Bug, who shot ahead.

"Go, Sally, go!" Bonnie cheered.

But Bug was too fast, and she crossed the finish line first.

As Sally crossed the finish line, Bonnie picked her up.

"You did great!" Bonnie said, giving her a big kiss. "And you'll always be a winner in my book."

In response, Sally gave Bonnie a big, wet kiss, too—right on her mouth!

CHAPTER 16
CELEBRATE GOOD TIMES!

"SALLY'S BIRTHDAY PARTY INVITE
is ready to go out," Bonnie said one night at
the dinner table.

"I just can't believe she's going to be a year
old," Emma said.

Bonnie nodded. "I'm just thankful every
day that she's healthy . . . and happy."

"Can I see the invitation?" Gavin asked.

"After dinner," Bonnie said. "You know the rule: no electronics at the dinner table. And this is going to be an e-invitation."

As soon as dinner was over and the dishes were washed and put away, the family settled into the living room. Bonnie pulled out her phone.

"Awww, this looks so cute!" Emma said.

"Come. Sit. Stay. As we celebrate Sally's First Birthday Paw-ty," Emma read.

"I love it," Brian agreed.

"Me too!" Gavin exclaimed. "But how long do I have to wait until the party?"

Bonnie laughed. "Have patience, my child," she said. "Have patience."

"Seriously, Mom," Gavin said.

"Well, the party is on December

seventeenth and today is December first," Bonnie explained.

Gavin thought for a moment and then groaned.

"Awww, sixteen days is too long to wait!"

"As I said, have patience, my child," Bonnie repeated.

The day of the party had finally arrived, and Emma was the first one in the family up.

She crept into her parents' bedroom and silently lifted Sally off their bed.

"We need to pick out your birthday outfit," Emma told her. "But first, I'll let you out."

After Sally came back inside, Emma whisked her away to her room. There, on her bed, Emma had laid out several outfits.

"We have a purple leopard one," Emma

began. "A blue lace one. And a pink fluffy one that comes with pearls and a matching pink party hat."

Sally let out a short, happy bark, and Emma giggled. "I guess it's the pink one!"

Once Sally was dressed, Emma led her down to the kitchen, where the family was having breakfast.

"Look at the birthday princess!" Bonnie said.

Emma beamed proudly, knowing how beautiful Sally looked.

"But Emma, her party isn't until this afternoon," Bonnie said. "At least take her party hat off for now."

Emma sighed, but she listened to her mother's suggestion.

At last, it was time to leave for the party, which was being held at the same dog-friendly restaurant where the Dodo had filmed Sally.

"Happy birthday, Sally!" Kat shouted as soon as Sally walked in.

Sally covered Kat with kisses.

"You don't know how happy I am to celebrate with you today," Kat said.

Sally looked around the restaurant. *The birthday princess has arrived! And I'm so glad everyone came to celebrate ME!* She ran around and greeted all her guests. *We are going to have the BEST time!*

Oh, some of my dog friends came, too! There's a poodle, a chihuahua, and oh, it's a Frenchie. Not sure how I feel about that one. But I can't wait to play. And eat. Oh look! There's a pup-cake just for me. Yummy, yum, yum! And presents, too! Toys! A comfy blanket. This is the Best. Day. Ever!

Eight days after Sally's birthday party, it was time to celebrate again, because it was Christmas.

Of course, Emma and Gavin were awake early that morning, eager to open the presents they found waiting for them beneath the tree.

"Look, Sally!" Emma said. "There are presents under the tree for you, too! Let's put on a red sweater and a Santa hat!"

After Emma got Sally dressed, she stepped back to admire her work.

"Now you have the Christmas spirit, Sally!" Emma said proudly.

"Jack, Zero, Bella, Ginger!" Gavin shouted. "There are presents under the tree for you, too!"

The four dogs scampered into the room and settled under the tree. But Sally was so excited she kept running around in circles. It seemed as if she couldn't wait to open her gifts.

Finally, Bonnie and Brian came down the stairs.

"What's all the racket?" Brian asked.

"*Dad*," Gavin began. "It's Christmas morning!"

"Oh, I forgot," Brian said with a grin.

"Can we open our gifts?" Emma asked eagerly.

"In a minute," Bonnie said. "First, I want to say that I am so thankful that I have this beautiful, loving family. And I am so thankful that Sally came into our lives. She helps make each day a little brighter, and she fills our lives with love!"

And with that, the entire family lifted imaginary glasses in the air.

"To Sally!"

EPILOGUE

THESE DAYS SALLY CONTINUES TO
go everywhere with her family: to work with
Bonnie, and to cheer and football practices
with Emma and Gavin. And, of course, she
goes out to eat at dog-friendly restaurants
around Houston and beyond!

Although the scarring in Sally's lungs will

never go away, she still *loves* to run. And when she's not running around at home with Zero, Jack, Bella, and Ginger, Sally is running in races.

In February 2023, Bonnie entered Sally in a toy breed race at a local restaurant that hosts dog races. A toy dog is very small, usually weighing less than fifteen pounds. So, Sally fit right in.

The day was cool, so Bonnie and Brian put on extra sweatshirts and headed out to the restaurant. But Sally didn't want to dress to impress—she just wanted to race!

Bonnie placed Sally behind the racing door and backed up down the field. As soon as the racing doors were opened, Sally bolted out.

"Come on, Sally!" Bonnie cheered from the finish line. "You've got this!"

And sure enough, Sally finished in first place!

However, in her second race, Sally wasn't so successful. But she was still a winner in Bonnie's eyes.

"You are the cutest dog ever," Bonnie said as she lifted up Sally for a cuddle and a hug.

I like to run, Bonnie! Sally thought. *When can I race again?*

Sally's next race wouldn't be until the fall.

"There's another wiener race in October," Bonnie told her family a few months later.

"Wow!" Brian said. "Are you going to enter Sally?"

"Definitely!" Bonnie told her husband. "She loves to race, and it's so much fun to cheer her on. I'll read to you what they say on their website: *'While the greyhound tends to get all the love when it comes to racing, we feel that there is another competitor whose lack of speed is more than* compensated by tenacity and spirit, the wiener dog!" I like the words *tenacity* and *spirit*. They describe Sally perfectly!"

Although it was October, the weather on the day of the race made it feel like the middle of summer. The first race was to be held at 2 p.m., and the temperature was expected to hit ninety degrees.

"Okay, Sally," Bonnie said as she placed her behind her gate at the start of the race. "It's hot today, so you just do your best!"

After securing Sally, Bonnie trotted over to the finish line to join her family.

"I hope she does well," Gavin said.

"Me too," Emma added.

"On your mark, get set, GO!" the announcer shouted.

With that, little legs raced down the track.

Ears flopped in the wind. Tongues hung from mouths.

"Go, Sally, go!" Bonnie shouted. "You can do it!"

Sally ran as fast as her little legs could carry her. And she crossed the finish line in third place.

Bonnie reached down and picked up Sally.

"Great job, Sally," she said. "You'll always be a *wiener* to us!"

Gavin and Emma giggled.

"Now, let's gather around for a hug," Bonnie said, embracing her kids and Brian.

The family squeezed together with Sally in the middle. And every single one of them could feel the love.

Especially Sally.

DACHSHUNDS MAKE GOOD PETS

Dachshunds are smart, playful, headstrong, and adventurous dogs. These dogs come in two sizes and three coats, with lots of colors and patterns. A standard dachshund is usually sixteen to thirty-two pounds. And a miniature dachshund only grows to about eleven pounds. The three types of coats are smooth-, wired-, and long-haired—just like Sally! Dachshunds can be many colors, from solid red or cream to a mix of black and tan to chocolate and tan, and many more! Some of the patterns on these dogs are called dapple (having spots or round patterns) and brindle (having black or chocolate stripes.)

If you're thinking about getting a dachshund as a pet, consider adopting a rescue like Sally! Here are some things you should know:

PERSONALITY:

One of the reasons dachshunds make great pets is because they are so friendly! They are also good for people living in apartments and small houses. Dachshunds are very social, and they just love being part of the family. But they do bark a lot, so be prepared!

HEALTH CARE:

Although dachshunds are small, they need lots of exercise to stay fit. It is important for them to build strong muscles to support their backs. Most dachshunds like to run, swim, and jump. But to help prevent injuries, a set of pet steps can help your dachshund easily reach tall beds or couches. It is also important to keep your dachshund at a healthy weight. If your dog gets too heavy, the extra weight will weigh them down and can possibly damage their spine or create knee problems.

FEEDING:

Dachshunds need to eat high-quality food that is appropriate for their age. For example, if you have a puppy, feed them puppy food! Puppies usually need to be fed three to four times a day. Older dogs can be fed twice a day. Try not to feed your dog food from the table, as it might upset their tummies. Just a warning: Dachshunds have an excellent sense of smell, so keep all food not meant for them out of reach!

TRAINING:

Dachshunds are very smart, but they can also be very stubborn. That means they can be hard to train. A good training method to use is called positive reinforcement. This means that toys or treats are used as a reward when the dog does something good. For dachshunds, reward-based training works much better than using harsh, loud commands.

GROOMING:

Since dachshund bellies are so close to the ground, they often need to be wiped down and brushed. And dachshunds also need their nails trimmed at least once a month. Smooth-haired dachshunds need the least grooming. Their coats can be wiped down with a glove, and they don't need a bath more than once every few months. But long-haired dachshunds (like Sally!) need to be brushed at least once a week to detangle their hair. Wire-haired dachshunds need their beards and eyebrows trimmed on a regular basis. And when brushing a dachshund, make sure to clean their ears. A lot of dirt can hide in there!

In general, dachshunds make great family pets, but every dog is an individual, so be sure any dog you're considering adopting gets along with every family member (human and furry!). With positive reinforcement training and lots of love, a dachshund can become an amazing family member!

WHY AND HOW TO ADOPT A RESCUE DOG

By adopting a dog from a rescue shelter, you are not only giving that dog a loving home, but you are freeing up space in that rescue for another animal. There are thousands of dogs living in shelters and rescues across the United States that are looking for homes. But before you decide to adopt, consider the following:

- First, discuss this with your family!
  - Talk about why you want to adopt a

dog. Do you love dogs? Does every member of your family feel the same way?

- Do you have enough space in your home? Is there a yard where the dog can run around? Can you easily and safely let the dog outside by itself? Or is there a place near your house where you can walk the dog? Is there a nearby park where the dog can safely run around?

- Do you have the time to take care of a dog? Remember, this is a full-time job! Will someone be home during the day to walk the dog? If not, can your family hire a dog walker, or have a friend or relative stop by? Do you have enough time between schoolwork and after-school activities to take care of and play with a dog?

- Are you ready to help train a dog? Training takes a lot of time and patience!

Once you and your family have decided that you want to adopt a rescue dog, what should you do next?

- Sit down at a computer or tablet with a family member to research local rescue organizations.
- Once you have found an organization, look at the available dogs.
- When you find some dogs you like that will fit your family's lifestyle, pay a visit to the rescue or shelter.
- You'll know when you find the perfect dog—it will be love at first sight!

MORE ABOUT THE BOTTLE BRIGADE

In 2019 Kathryn Mongrain was working twelve-hour shifts as a vet tech at an animal hospital. But Kat always found time to do more. In her spare time, she volunteered to bottle-feed abandoned puppies and kittens, and she also found the time to lend a helping hand to local animal rescue organizations. Still, Kat wanted to do more. So, she and her husband started The Bottle Brigade.

The Bottle Brigade's mission is to provide

special needs animals with medical care and rehabilitation. Once the animals are thriving on their own, The Bottle Brigade places these animals in loving homes.

Sometimes, the animals come in alone. Other times, they come in as siblings. One night, Kat got a call about two English bulldog puppies that needed her help. The brothers were born with cleft palates and couldn't feed on their own. Later that night, the pups arrived. Kat raced outside and rushed them into her nursery. Immediately, she could tell that they were having trouble breathing, because each time they took a breath, the air coming in and out of their lungs sounded very crackly. So, in addition to needing help eating, they needed help breathing, too! Kat got the pups set up with feeding tubes and put the babies in oxygen bubbles—just like she did with Sally!

When Kat had a moment to sit down, she decided on names for the brothers: Artichoke (Arti for short) and Salami (Sal for short.) Both Arti and Sal were very tiny. Within a few hours of being in the bubble, their noses started to turn pink. But they were so young that their eyes were still shut. Over the next few weeks, Sal seemed to be improving faster than his brother. Sal's eyes were open, and he was gaining weight. But little Arti wasn't doing as well. He needed extra medical attention, including a blood transfusion, and he had to spend more time inside his bubble than Sal.

Then one day, Arti opened his eyes! This was a sure sign to Kat that he was on the road to recovery. And as soon as Arti and Sal were healthy, they were off to their foster family.

Usually, Kat only takes in newborn animals. But one day, a breeder sent her a video of Phelps, a twelve-week-old pup with swimmer syndrome. His leg muscles hadn't developed properly, and so his legs splayed out, making him look as though he was swimming. (He was named after Olympic swimmer Michael Phelps!) Kat said that as she watched the video of Phelps, "his eyes were staring into my soul like he was begging for help." And although Kat knew that this puppy would need extensive physical therapy, she decided to take him in. She enrolled Phelps in a rehabilitation program. Each day, Kat dropped him off in the morning and picked him up at night. At the program, Phelps walked on a treadmill that was placed in a pool, and he also received massage therapy. To help him stand up, stretchy exercise bands were strapped between his legs. They helped keep Phelps's legs steady, and he was encouraged to walk. And step-by-step, Phelps improved. Soon he was walking all on his own!

Kat mostly gets calls to help cats and dogs. But one day, a call came in asking Kat to help a pig! Kat and Devin bottle-fed the pig, whom they named Toot, until he was ready to be adopted. Today, Toot lives as an indoor pig and enjoys air-conditioning and sleeping in bed with his humans!

Kat and her husband, Devin, have taken care of hundreds of animals in their home. But taking care of sick animals costs a lot of money. The organization is funded entirely through donations and fundraising. Some people make a one-time donation. Others contribute each month. Kat makes T-shirts for some of her animals, like the one she made featuring Sally. Then Kat and Devin sell the T-shirts online to earn extra money for the fur babies they care for. Plus, Kat uses some of the money she earns as a vet tech to buy supplies for the animals.

To help reach even more animals in need and the people who care for them, Kat created a Facebook Group for bottle feeders. There are people from all over the world in this group, including those who need help and those who can provide help. To learn more about The Bottle Brigade, visit their website at: www.thebottlebrigade.com.

ABOUT THE AUTHOR

BONNIE BADER has written more than fifty books for young people, including three books for The Dodo and six books in the Who Was? series. She was previously an editor and associate publisher, and she has developed and edited many bestselling book series for kids. Bonnie currently serves on the Advisory Council and as the publishing advisor for the Society of Children's Book Writers and Illustrators (SCBWI). When she isn't busy creating new stories, Bonnie enjoys teaching classes to aspiring authors and illustrators and visiting classrooms to share her love of reading and writing.

ABOUT THE BRAND

THE DODO is the world's #1 animal brand and the happiest corner of the Internet. They create fun, irresistible stories and products that help people feel connected to animals and learn how to be the best pet parents they can be. Their heartwarming content brings animal-loving kids and families (pets included!) closer together to feel all the feels.